Reading Skills

How to Read Better and Faster - Speed Reading, Accelerated Learning, Productivity

By: Nick Bell

Disclaimer

This document is geared towards providing exact and reliable information in regards to the topic and issue covered. The publication is sold with the idea that the publisher is not required to render accounting, officially permitted, or otherwise, qualified services. If advice is necessary, legal or professional, a practiced individual in the profession should be ordered.

- From a Declaration of Principles which was accepted and approved equally by a Committee of the American Bar Association and a Committee of Publishers and Associations.

The information herein is offered for informational purposes solely, and is universal as so. The presentation of the information is without contract or any type of guarantee assurance.

The trademarks that are used are without any consent, and the publication of the trademark is without permission or backing by the trademark owner. All trademarks and brands within this book are for clarifying purposes only and are the owned by the owners themselves, not affiliated with this document.

Introduction

Are you having problems reading your favorite novels? Do you simply love to read but simply aren't fast enough to read within a short time?

Would you love to read 10000 words per minute with 100% comprehension? Does this seem out of reach?

Well, it is not exactly out of reach as you may think. You can actually read all those magazines, newspapers and work files within just a few minutes.

This book teaches you how to speed-read. After reading this book, you will be in a position to read faster than you have ever imagined!

Reading this book will enable you learn important techniques to get you started on your journey to be a fast reader. After reading this book, you will finish that 30,000-word novel that you have been planning to read in less than 5 minutes.

About Speed Reading Simplified

This book will be broken down into several different sections to make reading much easier on you.

The first section is about how to make speed-reading work. While you can learn how to read fast, it is also important to ensure that you are effective in your fast reading; this is what this section is all about. The next section will look at the different things that usually happen when speed-reading. Finally, you get to learn of the specific techniques that will improve your reading.

The table of contents below will show you what is covered in this book.

Table of Contents

About Me

My name is Jessica Jacobs. I love reading novels, books, magazines and basically anything that can be read. My greatest challenge however, has been to read all that I want and still do other more important activities.

In my search for an effective way to read, I learned about Speed Reading. I compiled this book to show you the different techniques I used in order to read faster. Now I can read faster and even comprehend better. How cool is that?

Part 1:
Speed Reading 101

Did you know that it is possible to read more than 1000 words per minute with one hundred percent effective comprehension? Speed-reading is an old technique whose first concept was developed back in 1957. Even the then US president, John F. Kennedy, organized training classes for him and his family to learn how to read fast.

The most fascinating thing about speed-reading is the fact that you can increase your reading speed significantly from a mere 250 words per minute or 300 for college students, to an incredible 600 to 2000 words per minute. However, before starting, it is important to note that this is a gradual process, which takes some time to master.

Some Kids Could Read Faster Than You

Some studies suggest that children between the ages of 10 and 12 years have a higher comprehension rate than even adults, with some students skyrocketing their reading speeds to more than 3000 words per minute. Impressive, right? So it begs the question: why, then, don't parents invest in harnessing the reading speed of their twelve year olds?

There are three reasons for this: first, no one is willing to spend hundreds of dollars for their kids to learn how to speed-read the Cat and the Hare; there is simply no money for that. Secondly, most people are ignorant of this fact and thirdly, most of the available courses are designed with lots of paper work, which is, simply stated, too much for the kids. While it is true that children are quick learners, it is advisable to keep track of them when learning speed-reading to make sure that they internalize what they read in the first month. You can then monitor them for the next two months to see if they are using the technique on a regular basis.

What Dictates Your Speed in Reading?

The discrepancy in speed-reading and normal reading primarily stems from the way the reader reads, and the learning and thinking patterns that they apply when reading. A number of factors dictate the speed of a reader. These include:

- the nature of the content

- the natural ability of the reader to read fast

- the reading and comprehension skills that the reader has acquired

- the alertness of the reader

- his/her mental speed

- what the reader had for breakfast, and

- the amount of practice the reader has done, etc.

A fair speed for a beginner is around 600 words per minute, which is roughly double or nearly triple the normal speed. Speeds of more than 1000 words per minute require plenty of practice to achieve, but even 600 wpm is quite a remarkable speed that is extremely beneficial. One mistake most people make when beginning speed-reading is assuming that just because their brains seem to be aware of what they are reading, that they fully comprehend what they are reading. The truth is, just because your brain is aware of the information being processed, does not mean that you actually comprehend it or at the very least, you are going to remember it. One of the biggest weaknesses of reading fast is that it can deceive you that you have internalized and understood a text.

The reality is that there is no shortcut to memorizing something; it takes competence and proper learning strategies to store information in the long-term memory. Reading strategies are problematic when reading at high speeds and not everyone has the ability to apply speed-reading techniques alongside reading strategies successfully. In fact, no college speed-reading techniques suggest that reading and comprehending a text by just surfing through it once is easy, at best.

Speed Reading and Your Memory

When reading fast, your short-term memory is bombarded with information, leaving little or no time for the facilities of the long-term memory to fully grasp the information before it disappears. However, this gives you the opportunity to make split second decisions as to the value of the acquired knowledge, and the ability to slow down when you come across interesting or relevant text.

What most people do when trying to read fast is what could be said to be passive reading. This means that the reader passes over too much information with the hope that it will stick. This information strikes the brain like a fire extinguisher spray, giving it little time to sieve which information is relevant and which is not. Even before it can decide, more information is thrown its way into the cognitive circuitry to be processed.

Without proper comprehension skills, the brain is effectively squashed by the rapid speeds and loses the ability to understand or perceive relationships, or whether it understood an idea. In a nutshell, the only way to remember what you are reading is to find a purpose for it.

What most people fail to do when speed-reading is to organize the information they are reading fast enough to find a purpose for it. This means that no hooks are formed when reading to connect the data being received with the information already known to the reader.

Part 2:
Your Reading Speed Decoded

When you are reading a through text, several things happen. The rate of comprehension and the amount of time taken reading a certain passage depends primarily on the nature of the content. When you are reading an unfamiliar or complex concept, you tend to take a longer time looking at a particular word or groups of words, unlike when reading for pleasure. This is known as **fixation**, and takes roughly 0.25 seconds.

When this is done, you then proceed to the next word, and this process is called **saccade**, which takes about 1 second. After you repeat this once or twice, you then pause to internalize the phrase you just glanced at and this is called **comprehension**. This lasts between 0.3 and 0.5 seconds, averagely.

When you add all these comprehension gaps, saccades and fixations, you end up with the reading speed of ninety five percent of all college students, which is between two hundred and four hundred words per minute.

Aim for 'Speed Thinking'

So, if you want to speed up without losing comprehension, what should you do? Typically, speed-readers aim to shorten the length of time they take to **fixate** on a word. While virtually anyone can master the techniques used to gain speed while reading, very few people can use the proper thinking techniques to take the skill to the next level and make it count.

To achieve this, you have to develop visualization skills while reading in order to develop a thinking speed that is, at the very least, a notch higher than the speed of taking in words. You have to picture the words being processed like they are on white boards on your mind and using photographic albums to take notes and relay the information later on in an alternate version in your head.

The human brain can do this only through the visual processing hardware and the visual cortex, which has the right amount of physical neurons and speed to truly run this fast. Everything you will learn about memory and comprehension only attempts to reconstruct what you actively did with the information acquired and not what you actually saw.

As said earlier, if your goal is remembering things, there is no shortcut; one must use visualization thinking techniques to do it. While some people are born with this ability and can use it automatically when reading, others have to be coaxed into learning it while some people just have to force themselves into it. On the other side, certain people are just not cut out for it; they simply cannot learn it.

To be able to read at a pace of ten thousand words per minute, your brain actually produces around 400 distinct images in one second for which it has to distinguish and arrange the images in parallel. For this to happen, chances are that you are either at the autism level or show developed autistic traits, like half the people for which speed-reading actually works.

One method to use while learning speed-reading is to take the mindset of someone making a slide show presentation. Essentially, when you do this, the conscious part of your brain takes the concept of delivering a speech rather than scurrying through a text at a speed of light hoping that some words will stick to the long-term memory. Doing this normally involves you, as the reader going through a text using the normal speed reading technique at a fast rate and then learning how to read fast again completely from scratch. Doing this allows the information gathered to be processed in a slower, habituated but mostly unconscious level of the brain. With this modified version, rather than the center of attention being the incoming information, active cognitive processes involved in organizing the information become the focus of attention.

Part 3:
Advantages of Speed Reading

Reading makes up a large part of our lives. Students and business people especially have to go through a huge amount of reading material every day. So speed reading becomes really important for them. But while it is extremely useful for them, speed reading is not just meant for students and business personnel. It is equally beneficial to everyone, both in personal as well as professional life.

We all go through large amounts of data every day to get the important information that we need for smooth functioning. It can range from reading the newspaper to reading your school textbooks or articles on the internet. For this reason, it sounds sensible to invest some of your time into learning ways to help us in reading at a faster speed. If you look at it logically, spending considerably more time for the whole of your life by reading at your normal speed would be silly. Rather than doing that, you should take out some time out of your schedule to learn speed reading techniques, so that you can save up on your reading time on the whole.

Think of all the time it takes you going through your emails and social media news feeds. Now consider a scenario in which it takes you just half of that time to zip through your email inbox and social media feeds. Seems amazing, doesn't it? That's because it is, and not just because it saves time but also because it boosts your productivity.

But before you get carried away by the thoughts of reading at lightning fast speeds, you must ground yourself and remember that it takes some dedication and time to learn to speed read. This can make you averse to the idea. You may feel that this learning process is an unnecessary block of work load that you don't need to put on yourself. This happens when you think of learning almost any new skill, but you must keep your eyes set on the end goal, and not worry about the process. Think about the results it will achieve and how the little amount of extra time you will put in for a few weeks will help you save tons of time when reading later.

It is easy to feel that you don't really need to learn speed reading and that you can manage without it. Many people are unsure about this in the beginning, and if you are one of them, I have listed some of the biggest reasons why you shouldn't shy away from this idea and learn to speed read right now!

Liberation: Knowledge Creates Empowerment

This is a hard truth to accept, but people around you are always judging you, constantly, without fail. Your actions, your words, everything is being judged by others. People gain insights into your personality by your behavior, and any information you provide to them speaks something about you. It's a difficult life. And every time you hesitate or show reluctance to do something, people take it to be a sign of lack of knowledge. They may think that you are unsure about the facts. You lose credibility with your peers.

Reading gives you knowledge, and knowledge gives you the confidence you need to excel. When you completely understand something you read, you possess a great amount of knowledge that you can exhibit in the company of your peers, gaining respect from them, and also your superiors. At certain events, like parties, brainstorming sessions, or company meetings, you need to be good at thinking on your feet. Having intelligent and interesting conversation with a stranger can prove to be a really daunting task. You can only have opinions of your own when you are well read.

This is where speed reading steps in. If you are good at it, you can skim over important articles and headlines every day, thus staying up to date about the current topics. This helps you easily hold a conversation with people around you in a confident and self-assured manner. With knowledge, you feel liberated and superior.

Financial Security

Financial security is one of the most important things for people of today. If you are monetarily sound, you and your loved ones are economically and socially secure. As we already know, knowledge creates empowerment and helps you achieve goals in life. It can be a promotion or a new job, knowledge will pave the way for you.

Promotion requires you to be unique and better than your peers. You need to let your employers know that you are superior to your peers, and you can't do this by just going with the flow. The best way to stand out is to be more knowledgeable than the others. This can be done by reading a lot and through taking various courses. But the problem is the lack of time in our busy lives. This Herculean task doesn't seem so difficult once you are acquainted to speed reading.

Having an extra degree or a professional certificate adds to your credibility, and you become an eye candy to current as well as potential employers. It also gives you an edge over the competition, that is, your co-workers and other people with similar skill sets as you. Your overall value increases for the employer. This helps you move above in the hierarchy of your profession. Speed reading helps you gain more knowledge and juggle between learning and work without any additional stress.

Boost Your Self-Confidence

Are you the kind of person who breaks a sweat every time they need to address a crowd of seniors, peers and juniors? Are you comfortable with putting forward your opinions on things without any hesitation? Do you feel reluctant to share your thoughts with your boss?

Some of us do have confidence issues when faced with such tasks. But you won't face this issue if you are a knowledgeable person. If you understand your company's policies, analyze the competition and current market scene, study the effects of various factors on the stock market, and constantly work towards improving your skills, you won't feel hesitant to do any of the above mentioned things.

You will stop doubting yourself at every turn, and will radiate confidence strongly. This will help you put across your arguments and opinions on things without any reluctance. Your confidence will not only help in your personal growth but also in the overall development of your company as you will actively contribute in its improvement.

Speed reading will help you gain information from a wide variety of sources in a limited amount of time, and you will also be able to defend your opinions well before critics. Being well informed always feels amazing and empowering.

Enhanced Retention Abilities

Many people often confuse speed reading with just reading at a really great speed. But this is where they are mistaken. Speed reading is not solely about reading faster. It is about reading *better*. Speed is just one facet of this technique. The other one is completely and easily absorbing the information given in the text and being able to comprehend it quickly. Speed reading aims to make us more *efficient* readers, not just faster readers.

Retaining a particular bit of information becomes much easier when you understand it fully. If you just mug up a fact, you won't remember it a few weeks later, but if you take the time to understand a concept and its working, you will probably remember it for years to come.

Speed reading improves your retention abilities, and this improved memory helps you in all walks of life. It is believed that memory also affects creativity and innovation.

Improved Learning Abilities

Concentrating fully on the task at hand can be difficult for us many times. It doesn't matter whether it's a minor assignment or a full-blown PowerPoint presentation, we easily get distracted and find new ways to procrastinate our work.

Speed reading comes to our rescue at this point. It helps a person focus at a task and makes it difficult to get distracted. Speed reading has an inherent advantage and that is speed. When you are reading quickly, there is less chance of being distracted. Your interest level also surges up and stays high. You will always feel more eager to read and gain more knowledge with speed reading. This will increase your prospects on both personal and professional levels.

Critical Thinking

It is an old saying that the human brain is like a sponge. It has great capabilities to absorb information you feed to it. The brain adapts itself and rearranges information quickly as the need arises. We call this ability the neuroplasticity of brain.

This neuroplasticity is positively affected by speed reading. New pathways and connections are created more easily in the brain and the information provided gets stored faster and with much more ease. What this means for you is that your ability to think critically and make new connections between things improves dramatically. Speed reading helps you be more logical, reason better and create meaningful links between things you learn so you can recall things easily in a real life situation.

Stress Reduction

Information comes to us in many different ways, and this is one of the reasons why we try to multi-task to gain information from multiple sources. Surely you are familiar with going through your social media feed while watching the TV, or keeping an ear open for the gossip at office while preparing your presentation.

This creates a diversion for your mind, and your attention span decreases. You become incompetent at what you do, and many times, you even miss out on important information from all sides because you weren't paying full attention to anything. Fragmented focus doesn't help anyone.

Speed reading helps you focus at one thing at a time and doesn't let your attention stray away. This has a bit of a meditative effect on your brain, and you feel the stress on your mind and body reducing. You feel relaxed and at peace.

Heightened Sense of Ambition

Speed reading endows you with not just a fast reading speed, but a lot of other abilities as we have discussed earlier. And when you have improved memory, more creativity, better reasoning, and enhanced focus, you will automatically feel a heightened sense of ambition. You will want to achieve more with your improved abilities.

You move ahead in your life with a lot more confidence when your abilities are improved, and this, in turn, increases your enthusiasm for doing new things and achieving new horizons. You move up in your career at a greater pace.

Innovation and Transformation

The art of bringing a change and taking an idea or thought to create something of value is known as innovation. We have already discussed how speed reading makes you more creative and think on a higher plane. This can help you be a more innovative person. You, as a thought leader and an innovator, can revolutionize an idea or product, and come up with something truly brilliant during brainstorming sessions.

The qualities of a good innovator include being knowledgeable, well-read, creative, and focused. And speed reading is known to increase all of these qualities. So it is an added benefit for you as a speed reader. You can be more innovative and transform an idea into something of real worth.

Superior Problem Solving Skills

Facing problems and challenges is a part of every individual's daily life. It can be any sort of problem, relating to profession or personal life, big or small. Something that plays a vital role in solving these problems is our subconscious mind. It is much more efficient at solving problems than the conscious mind, over a hundred times faster!

Speed reading helps us take in and comprehend larger chunks of information in a shorter span of time. This can be used to our advantage while trying to solve a problem. We can constantly feed our brain with lots of information and flood our subconscious with it. At this rate, the subconscious will attempt to solve the problems at double the normal speed.

In this manner, you will only take half an hour to solve a problem which might ordinarily have taken an hour or more. You won't have to stay awake all night worrying about your problems. You would solve it quickly and stay stress free.

Part 4:
Is Reading Second Nature?

Though we may be unaware of it, reading takes a major part of our daily activities. From the office to our home and vice versa, there is not a single moment in our life that we will not be presented with something to read; from the mail that just arrived to our mail box, our favorite health fitness magazine, the daily newspaper, to the workload in our place of work. Even while driving, our eyes are always scanning the road for posters and billboards for something to read. What's more, a great share of our time is spent surfing the internet for information, whether we are researching for a new herb to plant in our garden or we are just passing through our favorite social media, looking through the updates from our friends.

Since we already acquired the skills to read and write before the age of ten, we naturally assume that we are good readers, right? Wrong. When we think of it, reading is the work related skill most people use. However, it is also a skill that most of us take for granted once we reach the age of twelve. After all, we often assume since we can read some textbooks and understand them, we are a good reader. Maybe not!

Given the fact that reading takes a substantial amount of our time, we can benefit from this skill when we improve it. So the question is; what does good reading entail? What is the difference between how we read and speed-reading and what can you do to transition onto the other side?

How Does the Brain Read?

When you think about it, reading is quite a complex skill. Have you ever sat down and thought about what happens when you are reading? How does your brain associate one word with the other to construct meaningful sentences? Research has shown that during reading, your eyes are fixated on two separate characters, and not one. Your brain then internalizes these words and focuses to make sense out of them. This process happens almost instantaneously, as you surf through pages and pages of information. Like any book lover will testify, while reading a book for pleasure, say a novel, your brain comes alive with emotions and images, and your senses are even turned on. Sounds romantic, I know, but there is concrete evidence to support this notion, which means that these things actually happen to your brain. When reading, you can actually change your brain's structure, become empathetic, and you can even trick your brain into thinking that you have experienced only what you have read in novels.

When reading, even without being prompted, you make photos in your mind. This normally happens when you are reading such books as novels and other material with vivid imagination, making it a fun process that can allow you to create another world in your mind.

This can also happen without intention. Research has shown that reading content that has a visual description makes it easier to identify photos of such objects easily, suggesting that when you read sentences, you automatically bring up images of objects in your mind. Did you know that your spoken word can also liven up your brain and put it to work?

Despite several critics on the subject, research has proven that you can actually light your brain up with the mere act of just listening to a story. When someone narrates a story to you, both the parts that process language in your brain and the experiential parts are activated. When you hear something related to food, your sensory cortex activates, while your motor cortex is activated by motion. Interestingly, this process is not limited to reading or listening to audios. In fact, majority of our conversations are filled with gossips and personal stories, which is actually a good thing as it has been shown to be good exercise for your brain. So go ahead and listen as your co-worker drawls about how their vacation was, listen to an audio book on your way to work or tune to talk radio. It is good for the brain!

The most fascinating thing about the human brain is the fact that when you are reading, or when someone tells you something he/she experienced, your brain treats the information as if you actually lived it in real life. In other words, it is almost the same thing as living the experience. There is a perfectly reasonable explanation for this; your brain actually believes that you experienced the story. Whether you are reading something or experiencing it, the same neurological regions of your brain are stimulated. Simply, novels have the ability to enter into our feelings and thoughts.

Any type of reading can stimulate your brain, but there is a difference in the thinking pattern for every reading style. This means that there are varying benefits with each type of reading, as all of them provide different experiences. For instance, close literary reading stimulates complex cognitive functions in your brain, while reading for pleasure increases blood flow to different parts of your brain. If you look at it that way, reading a novel for literally purposes and considering its value can effectively work out your brain with more benefits than merely pleasure reading.

Improving the Brain Function

One of the most effective ways that have been shown to have a significant impact on the brain is learning a new language. Research has shown that learning a new language can cause a significant growth in the cerebral cortex and hippocampus parts of your brain, depending on the level of effort applied. So pick up a foreign language course book and start learning. You will be amazed by the results; it's a good workout for your brain!

Moreover, with the advance in technology today, e-books are very popular on the internet. This has caused growing concerns among many people as to the degree of adjustment from the traditional hard copy books to the internet eBooks. However, experts have dismissed these concerns, claiming that the human brain can take an approximate one-week (seven days) to get used to eBooks. Therefore, despite your age or the length of time you have been reading on paper, your brain can adapt to this new technology very fast. In fact, it takes an average of seven days for your brain to adapt to any new technology, even e-reading!

However, while it takes a short time for your brain to adapt to new technology, this does not in any case suggest that it has the same benefits accrued from reading on paperback. In particular, e-books lack what experts call spatial navigability. These are the physical cues, such as the number of pages left for you to complete the book that give you a sense of location. Evolution has taught us to depend on location cues to navigate our way around, without which we would be left with a feeling of being lost in some way. However, when you add such physical cues as page numbers and percentage read, e-books can give a similar physical experience as that of a paper back.

The structure of a story enables our brain to think in sequence, inflating our focus spans. All stories have a starting point, middle, and a conclusion, and this is a good thing. This structure enables our brains to think in sequence, thereby associating cause with effect. Your brain's ability to think in this pattern increases with the more books your read. In fact, you are encouraged to take this knowledge and use it on your kids to read to them as often as you can. This installs the story structure in their young minds when their brains have better plasticity and the ability to increase their attention span.

Are Good Readers Born or Made?

It is important to note that not everyone is a born reader. Some people are just naturally poor readers. However, while these people might not truly appreciate the value of literature, it is possible to change the structure of their brain by training them to become better readers. One important thing to note is that, at the end of the reading program, when conducted efficiently, the volume of the white matter of the brain increases significantly. Furthermore, it has been proven that you can improve the structure of your brain by incorporating consistent healthy reading habits. The feeling one gets when you get lost in a book is out of this world, and by doing so, you can actually change the physical structure of your brain.

When reading a book and you let go of the mental and emotional chatter of the real world, you enjoy the benefits of deep reading, and you can even experience what the characters are feeling. Doing this makes more empathetic of the people in the real world and allows them to be more sensitive with the lives of others.

Activating the Five Senses Through Reading

It has long been known that the language regions of the brain, such as Wernicke's area and Broca's area, are involved in the process of written word interpretation. What was recently discovered was that, our brains are activated by narratives in so many areas as well, explaining why the process of reading can feel so lively. When you come across words like soap, cinnamon and lavender, for instance, not only is the region that processes language in our brain activated, but also the sensory cortex that deal with smells.

Interestingly, how your brain deals with metaphors is also remarkable. When you hear metaphors that are used on a regular basis such as "a rough day" which are very familiar, your brain treats them like any other words and does not respond any different. On the other hand, when you read a metaphor concerning touch, the sensory cortex of your brain involved in touch is activated. Similarly, metaphors such as "the artist had a velvet voice" and "the undertaker had leathery hands" are bound to rouse your sensory cortex, but common phrases such as "the artist had a pleasing voice" and "the undertaker had strong hands" might not. Words related to motion have also been found to activate parts of the brain other than the language processing areas. For instance, words like "he grasped the object" and "she kicked the ball" are bound to cause activity on the motor cortex of your brain associated with body movements.

The concept with which the brain internalizes narrative content has been subject of studies for many years. The brain does not seem to be able to distinguish between fictional reading and real life experience. This has largely been attributed to the assumption that the human brain simulates a vivid reality when reading, a reality that runs on a reader's mind in the same way that a computer runs computer simulation. The thing about fiction is that it contains imaginative metaphors, malodorous details, and conscientious descriptions of people and their actions, which offers an almost exact replica of real life experience. As such, the novel provides an unequaled medium to explore the human social and emotional life and it has been shown that just as the brain responds to depictions of textures and smell, so does it treat fictional characters' interactions like social encounters of real life.

The Theory of the Mind

The brain contains a significant overlap between the brain networks that comprehend stories and those that navigate our interactions with other individuals, more so in interactions where we try to figure out other people's emotions and thoughts. Scientists even have a name for this ability of the brain to construct maps defining other people's intentions. They call it the **theory of the mind**.

One of the benefits of narratives is that they give us the rare and unique opportunity to make use of this capacity as we try to empathize with the frustrations and longings of the characters, speculate at their hidden motives, and monitor their encounters with friends and foes, lovers and neighbors. In simple terms, reading is an exercise that enables us to hone our interactive social skills. In fact, studies have shown that individuals who often read fiction have a better ability to understand other people, identify with their feelings, and see the world from their view. Another thing about fiction that makes it particularly important is the fact that it allows us to effectively negotiate the social world, which is a very tricky process that requires us to weigh countless interactions of cause and effect. Just like computer simulations allow us to analyze complex complications such as forecasting the weather or flying a plane, so do novels, dramas and stories help us comprehend the sophistications of social life. You have always heard experts preach that reading novels improves and enlarges us as human beings. Now you have brain science that proves this truer than you would have ever imagined!

Part 5:
Speed Reading Obstacles

Learning to read at a speed of 600 words per minute and above is an interesting experience, but imagine reading at a skyrocketing speed of 25,000 words per minute! You will be able to read a book in five minutes, which normally takes almost a day or more to finish. At this rate, you will finally be able to get rid of the clutter of files on your desk, both at the office and at home. What's more, you will have the advantage of saving time, engage in multiple activities, and reduce work-related stresses. Moreover, when you are able to finish reading all the materials for your work, you can then indulge in storybooks, novels, and other pleasure reading materials. However, as much as this is possible, certain things need to change in order to effectively maximize this ability.

Old Reading Habits and Beliefs

For starters, you need to change your old fashioned ways of thinking and adapt a modern and sophisticated strategy of involving the whole brain; in particular, the right hemisphere of the brain. Most people find it hard to incorporate speed-reading for a number of reasons, the most common one being the fact that most people do not believe that this is possible.

This is hard to change, as it was hardwired in our system since childhood and we were taught that the only way we could read a book is by focusing on it word by word. This is quite logical given the fact that you need to engage your conscious memory in order to remember facts when you are reading. What you do not know is that you do not have to engage your conscious level of the mind when reading for you to remember information. A much more complicated system that requires making use of the whole mind can help you master information and remember it efficiently. This is what enthusiasts of neuro-linguistic programming apply. The technique gives you the ability to link your subconscious and conscious levels of the brain while reading to:

1. Read through a text at a glorious speed

2. Retrieve the information learned from the subconscious mind to the conscious level of the mind.

When you do this efficiently, the results are tantalizing. With a maximum speed of 25,000 words per minute, you can match your reading speed with a comprehension rate of up to 75 percent. Let's look at the obstacles that hinder efficiency while practicing speed-reading?

Fixation Speed

One of the barriers to effective speed-reading is the time taken to move your eye from one word to the next in order to make constructive sense of the passage, also known as fixation. While reading, your eyes move from word to word, as you are doing right now, and stop at every word to read it. The approximate time taken to fixate on a given word is determined by its complexity and familiarity to the reader. If you are a normal (average) reader, you will take 10 fixations to read 10 words, meaning that you will be reading the text word by word. A fast reader, on the other hand, will take roughly 4 to 5 stops for the ten words. The difference is obvious; a fast reader has fewer fixations.

Regression

Another obstacle to effective speed-reading is looking back over the text you have already read, a habit known as regression. Most of the time, this happens intuitively. You run your fingers back over a certain word or phrase in order to get a clearer meaning. While most people do this for unfamiliar phrases and words, sometimes it gets habitual, looking back over even simple phrases that are easy to comprehend. The setback in doing this is that it reduces your reading rate, and is a waste of time as well.

Sub-Vocalization

Another hindrance to effective reading is sub vocalization; the act of hearing or saying words while reading silently. This normally happens in the brain and is a habit that most of us are guilty of. When reading a text, you subconsciously tend to repeat the words in your mind. The fact is, when you do this, you tend to limit your ability to read fast because you cannot read and speak at the same time effectively. There is a very huge difference between reading and speaking in terms of speed. When reading and speaking, the speed at which you complete a text is limited to about 150 to 200 words per minute, the average reading speed of a normal (average) person. However, what you did not know is that if you eliminate these voices in your head and concentrate on the text you are reading, you could read at a staggering speed of 10,000 words per minute. And that's not all. When you do it effectively, you can even increase your rate of comprehension. Think about it. Imagine how many doors this technique would open for you. You could earn your degrees faster, finish your work reports on time, manage your time effectively and so much more.

Breaking the Bad Habits

It all starts with breaking the bad habits.

How to Stop Sub-Vocalization

In order to break sub-vocalization, you need to determine first how often you do it. Admittedly, everyone does this to some degree. It is not an easy habit to stop. This is especially because, when the ancient Normans and Anglo-Saxons invented the language, they had no listening devices or MP3s. Written word was designed to convey message over long distances where you could not shout. As such, it was like speaking directly to someone. That is why we naturally tend to read out text, either with our lips or with our minds. When grouped according to vocalization, there are three different types of readers:

Motor Readers

Motor readers tend to speak the words they are reading using their tongues, and sometimes move their voice cords while trying to sound out the words. These are the slowest readers there is, with a snail pace of 150 to 200 words per minute. In addition, these readers have the slowest comprehension rate relative to the reading speed. This is mainly attributed to their slow reading speed.

Auditory Readers

Auditory readers, on the other hand, do not speak out the words as they read them. However, they tend to repeat the words silently, and their speed range is between 200 and 400 words per minute. These readers are extremely skillful, and have a comprehensive vocabulary meaning that they can recognize complex words quickly.

Visual Readers

Visual readers are the most outstanding of all. These readers have minimal or null vocalization. They do not say or hear words as they read them. They also tend to have the highest reading and comprehension rates, sometimes escalating to a mountain high 25,000 words per minute. The main reason for the success of these readers is the fact that they read ideas when surfing a text, rather than individual words, which is what makes the difference.

In order to drive the point home, take the example of speaking to a friend. When a friend is describing something to you, what normally happens? Do you hear his words as he speaks, or do you visualize his descriptions, ideas and thoughts? Of course, when someone speaks, all you hear are words. The difference is how you interpret the message. You visualize how he went to Comoros for vacation, the people he met, his encounters, and so on. The same goes for reading. The purpose of reading is to get a meaning of what the writer is saying, not to hear the sound. When you see a word on text, you visualize what it means by skipping the vocalization. You don't interpret words as words but instead interpret them as units of meaning, thoughts, ideas and descriptions.

How to Stop Vocalization

If you want to **stop vocalization**:

Keep Your Mouth Busy

Try keeping your mouth busy during the reading process. You could chew gum, eat something or place a pen or pencil between your mouth to keep you distracted. When you begin, you will find it hard to concentrate as you move your eyes from word to word. However, as you get used to it, you will find yourself reading faster without using the pen or chewing gum. Most readers in the motor stage break the habit of moving their lips as they read within a short time after trying these techniques.

Visualize

Rather than seeing the words, try to perceive them. Picture the words as symbols, each with a hidden meaning. Next, imagine your ears are fixed with a volume control and turn down to the mute. Widen your peripheral vision. When you do this, you will be able to take in more text, read more words, and consequently reduce vocalization while reading. Imagine the words are thought units in sentences when you are reading. Therefore, when interpreting the text, think of the sentences as continuous thought units that convey to give a meaning, instead of word sequences.

Concentrate

Lastly, improve your concentration when you are reading. Much of reading fast effectively stems from concentrating harder than you previously used to.

How to Prevent Regression When Reading

The term regression is used to describe the habit of re-reading words from a passage in a bid to understand the meaning. Majority of the people who do this are normally unaware of their habit. They do this because they lack confidence in the understanding of the read text, so they feel that they have to go over it again in order to comprehend. However, this practice is sometimes required in certain scenarios like in reading a dry manual or academic paper. On the other hand, some authors are partly to blame for this practice. Reading is an association between the reader and writer; but when the writer does not hold his end of the bargain, you are left with no option but to regress in order to figure out what the heck is happening. Of course, regression is hazardous in that it slows you down, wastes time, and reduces your ability to comprehend. If you regress compulsively, you can do something about it.

Whenever you feel the urge to regress when reading a text, resist the temptation by doing the exact opposite. Eventually, you will find that you do not need to regress in order to improve your understanding. If you find regression an especially thorny obstacle to handle, you can try this exercise to help you out. Find a piece of paper or any material that is as long as the text you are reading. When reading, cover the parts where you are done reading with the paper or desired material to avoid going back over the text. This way, the past lines will not be visible to you, meaning that you will not regress.

Fixating on Eye Fixations

For you to see anything clearly, you must hold your eyes still on the direction of the object. Whether you want to observe the highest peak on a mountain, a fly, someone passing by, or anything else, your eyes need to be still, otherwise everything will be blurry. The same principle applies in reading. In order to grasp what you are reading, your eyes need to fixate on every single word, but you also have to move them in order to capture the subsequent word, for you to make sense of the passage. The question is; how can you fixate your eyes and make them move at the same time? This is where eye fixations come in. When reading, your eyes focus on a single word or group of words; then take some time for you to grasp and when you have comprehended, move to the next words.

For many years, people took advantage of the fact that everybody at some time reads a text one word at a time. Researchers assumed that fast readers took a shorter time to fixate on a single word than normal readers did, which explains the disparity in the speeds. In addition, if you can conduct a test with a friend to observe the movement of their eyes as they read a text, you will notice that the eyes move by fits and starts, as opposed to a steady pace across the page. When you are reading, there are some words that might require extra attention than others, thereby increasing the period of fixation of that word. When you add the general sum total of the length of time of fixation a normal reader uses, and that of a fast reader, you will notice that the latter has fewer eye fixations than the previous.

Expand Your Vocabulary

One way of reducing the time you take to fixate with a certain text is to expand your vocabulary. The problem with having a limited vocabulary of words is that, when you come across a word you are not familiar with, you tend to take a longer time trying to internalize it in a bid to figure out what it means.

Familiarize With The Subject

Eye fixation is also determined by the familiarity of the text to the reader. If you find that the material you are reading is relatively new, chances are that it will take you a longer time to finish reading the text. On the other hand, if you are familiar with the passage, you will take a shorter time.

Part 6:
Techniques Used In Speed Reading

The following techniques are used in speed reading:

Skimming

Skimming is a technique used mostly to get a general idea of what the text is all about. To do this, rather than reading the whole text, you scan over the whole passage to get the main ideas. These are usually found primarily in the first and last paragraphs, and in the first sentences of all the paragraphs. It is also useful to observe how the text is organized.

When skimming through a text, it is sometimes advisable to first read the passage in detail in order to activate the knowledge you have about the information contained in the text. Since reading is an interactive process, you will need to start constructing its meaning using the marks made on the paper. This will require your full attention throughout the reading process.

Skimming a text to get a general idea of what it is all about can help you formulate questions to keep you alert. When using the skimming technique, you can increase your reading ability significantly. People who use skimming when reading do it to get a general idea of what the material is about, rather than reading over the whole thing.

The Pros

Skimming allows you to read more content in a shorter time. It works best when looking for main or general ideas, and is best suited for nonfiction materials.

Skimming is useful for a number of reasons.

1. For starters, you can use it when going through a text you have already read.

2. Secondly, you can use it to read material that for any number of reasons does not require detailed attention.

3. Thirdly, this technique has an added advantage over simple previewing in that it can give you a more vivid image as to what the text is about, before reading it again.

The Cons

While skimming is a useful tool that helps to identify the main ideas in a text, it tends to reduce the overall understanding of the reader. This is mainly because it does not involve the whole context but only the relevant details that are useful to the reader.

Unfortunately, many people get the whole concept of skimming wrong. Of course, skimming involves scanning over a text to extract the main points but it does not mean placing your eyes anywhere they fall.

How to Use Skimming to Your Advantage

To do skimming effectively, you have to design a structure that does not involve you reading everything. However, keep in mind that what you read should be more relevant than what you leave out. The question is; what material should you keep and which ones should you leave out?

Say, for example, you are doing a research on a website or a long chapter. How do you go about it? The first thing you need to do is to read through the first paragraphs in detail to get a hang of what the text is about. Once you know where it is headed, you can then start reading the first sentences of each paragraph only. Otherwise known as topic sentences, these first sentences give the reader the main idea of a paragraph.

If you do not get the idea behind a topic sentence, or if you find the topic interesting, you might need to skim more. Once you are done reading the first sentence of a paragraph, you should scan through the rest of the paragraph looking for any important pieces of information such as dates, names, or events. Continue skimming through the text, doing the same for each paragraph until you get to the last few paragraphs.

The last paragraphs are usually detailed with a conclusion or summary, so it is best to stop skimming there. Since skimming filters certain information, it is better to read in detail the last paragraphs of the text. If you find that you are grasping the main ideas from the topic sentences, then you are doing it right.

When Should You Use Skimming?

Since skimming is done at a fast speed, and involves less than usual comprehension, you should not use it all the time. However, skimming can also be very useful in many areas. Take for example, an instance where you are required to make a presentation on the advancement to the first trip to space. When carrying out your research, you come across a pile of books and a couple of articles on the topic. Since you are short of time, and you cannot read everything to the end, what do you do? Skimming can help you scan over all the documents in a short time, and get a significant amount of solid information on the subject.

Moreover, you are more likely to use more materials for your research to get usable information. Perhaps you have an exam the next day and are not quite prepared. Through skimming, you can scan over the text you have already read, locate the details you have not yet mastered and study that material only.

Some Tips Before You Skim

There are a couple of questions you should ask yourself when you want to skim over a given text.

1. How much time do you have to read over the text, and how long is it?

2. Have you read the text before?

3. Is the text fictional or non-fictional?

4. Are there parts of the text that can be skipped?

If you find that there are parts of the text that you don't need to read, or you already have an idea about, you can skip it. Just because someone wrote something, you are not under an obligation to read it. You can scan over the text and pick up what is relevant then leave the rest. If you hit the nail on the head and skim only the information you need, overriding what is unnecessary, you will be surprised at the amount of information you can acquire in a very short time.

Scanning

A closely related technique to skimming is **scanning**. The main difference between skimming and scanning is that, with skimming you read through the text looking for relevant information, while in the latter, you preview the text to get specific information or facts about something. Examples of situations where you can use scanning is when looking for a friend's address in a directory, looking for your favorite show in a cable guide, or when you want to know the sports scores from the newspaper.

The Proper Way to Scan

To scan effectively, you need to know how the information you are scanning is structured, and understand what you read in order to locate the specified details. The best thing about scanning is that it enables you to locate information and any details you need in a hurry. Since you already use scanning in your day-to-day activities, a little information about it may come in handy.

Some of the main factors to consider when scanning:

- Your purpose for scanning

- Where the information is located

- How it is structured.

Tips to Scan Quickly

A text can be arranged in different ways. It could be arranged alphabetically, non-alphabetically, chronologically, textually or by category. Information arranged alphabetically starts from A-Z, while chronologically arranged information follows numerical or time order. Most people using scanning to find some information usually use their hands to locate the details. What do you do with your hands when looking for a word in the dictionary? Do you scan your fingers through the calendar when looking for a meeting time, or when reading a bus or train schedule?

When scanning, running your hand over the text you are reading is extremely beneficial in terms of focusing your attention, and keeping in place when reading a column of text. You can also use your peripheral vision when you want to maximize your scanning results. When reading over a text, your eyes tend to overlook what you are scanning and can see some details over and below your text. Take advantage of this when searching for information. You should always have your keywords in mind when scanning over a material. For instance, when surfing the time schedule for a train going to New York City from Washington DC, what you need to be looking for in the text is "from Washington DC" and "to New York City".

The purpose of scanning is to get specific details about a certain subject. Perhaps you want to get some information about a topic you are researching about. How do you go about it? Here, you can apply scanning by running over the indexes of books, documents, reference materials and websites, to find out if the materials contain the information you need and in what pages you can locate them.

Most people use scanning without being aware. Now that you have this information, you can use it effectively, and in more instances than one. In most cases, some of the information contained in a text is irrelevant, and it helps to be able to scan, skim and skip that information. Of course, this skill, like all others, gets better with practice. The more you do it, the more you can use it effectively and benefit from it.

Meta Guiding

If you have ever seen someone speed read over a text, chances are you were amazed by the rate at which the reader seemed to be running their fingers over the text while their eyes followed suit. This is what Meta guiding is. It involves drawing invisible shapes when reading over a column of information in order to broaden the visual context of the information being received, and increase the rate of comprehension while reading at lightning speeds.

The best thing about **Meta guiding is it reduces sub-vocalization**, the act of repeating out words as we read them. One set back of sub-vocalization is that it slows down the rate of comprehension and reading by including speaking in your reading. In order for reading and comprehension to be fully effective, you need to stop repeating the words you read in your mind. This is because, when you do this, you reduce the rate of reading to approximately the same as that of speaking. The speed of reading, as you know, should be much faster than the speed at which you speak. Therefore, when you separate the two, you can reap significant benefits in terms of reading and comprehension. Visualizing is also an important part of this technique.

Visualization

When reading over a text, one of the most effective ways of ensuring that we hold on to the information for a longer period than usual is visualization. This technique involves creating mental images in our minds as we read over a given material. The human brain is hardwired to remember memorable things, rather than informational details. That is why it easier to remember a story you read ten years ago, but you cannot recall what you learned in your biology class a couple of years back. For this reason, many teachers and students use visualization to apply a similar concept used in pleasure reading to master informational text.

Visualization strengthens the comprehension skills of the reader by using the words in the text to create mental images, which act as hooks to extract the information being learned from long-term memory. When visualizing, several things happen. The idea behind this concept is using the words you are reading to relate with past life experiences using imagery in order to make the content more memorable. People who use visualization techniques normally have a better ability to recall things than those who don't. When you do it effectively, this technique will not only improve your comprehension rate, but your reading speed as well. When reading over a material, relate the information with the movies, television shows, paintings, pictures, photographs, places you have been, people you have met, and such experiences to get a vivid picture of what the writer is saying.

The Ruler as a Tool for Speed Reading

The simplest method used in Meta guiding and Visualization is running a finger through the sentences as you read over a text. As you do this, you can swiftly underline the passages or sentences you view relevant imaginarily as you progress. One tool that can come in handy is a ruler. With this, you can kill two birds with one stone. The ruler can be used a mental guide to keep you focused as you are reading, and to hide the already read words.

In addition, doing this can also help you avoid what most readers subconsciously do: **regression**. This is caused by re-reading a text by going over the words again. If you are reading something from the screen, such as this book from the internet, you already have the advantage of a ready visual guide: your mouse cursor. By using the pointer to read over text, you can increase your reading speed on screen too.

Speed Reading Software

When most people think about speed-reading, the first thing that comes to mind is speed. After all, you are learning about improving your reading speed, aren't you? While to some extent this is true, speed-reading is not all about increasing the rate at which you read a text to 3 or 4 times faster. It is also about making use of the information learned. Understandably, many people make a mistake of assuming this notion when trying to increase their reading speeds. But really, what more would you gain if you were able to read over text at a speed of 1000 words per minute and you did not comprehend a thing?

Most of the techniques explained above involve getting rid of the poor reading habits many people use while reading and incorporating new ideas to improve the reading speed. This section is a little bit different as it involves using software to improve reading ability, with a better comprehension rate. There are a number of computer programs designed to improve the speed and comprehension of readers. Some of the programs present information in a serial stream, mainly because the brain uses such a serial stream to break down information before processing and interpreting it. These programs are best suited for boring information, so to speak, such as reading the news, or such things as email that do not require complete comprehension. Some of the programs include:

Spreed

You can use this software to read any text online. This is a Chrome extension that uses the RSVP method to flash words on the screen of your computer. All you have to do is pick the text of your choice from any site on the internet and Spreed simplifies it. One of the advantages of this program is that it tries to eliminate sub-vocalization, repeating words in your mind, thereby increasing the speed of reading. When using Spreed, you first highlight the text you want, then right click on it and select "Spreed the text". As soon as you do this, a pop up will appear on the screen with a speed-reading app, which will ask you to click "play". Spreed will then start running through all the words in the text. You can modify the font, number of words and the speed in order to make it easier to read.

OpenSpritz

This recently unveiled application claims to enable you speed-read a novel in ninety minutes. When using OpenSpritz, you can read any document online by modifying the speed. The article then appears on the screen, displayed word by word. The main idea behind this program is to **minimize saccades**, the tiny movements your eyes make as you read over text from word to word to make sense of it. While most speed reading techniques emphasize on the **elimination of sub-vocalization**, OpenSpritz is structured grammatically, with the inclusion of commas, full stops and such punctuation marks that gives it a better flow when read with sub-vocalization. Moreover, the program is built completely in Javascript, meaning that no web page on the internet cannot work with it. To extract content, it uses Readability API, and can work with the currently selected text.

Syllable/Velocity/Outread

These iOS applications use different speed reading techniques to help you improve your reading speed. Outread uses a modification of meta guiding, while both Syllable and Velocity use a variation of RSVP.

Quantum Speed Reading

This relatively new technique was first developed in Japan and has been used to enable reading documents very fast. The most fascinating thing about Quantum speed-reading is the fact that you do not need to open the book while reading it. Interesting, right? Given especially the fact that most of us learned that the only way to read a book is to peruse through its pages, this new technique is *simply amazing*. During this process, the book is placed in front of the reader and the pages flipped quickly in the same way that a pack of cards is shuffled. Truly, this is quite a remarkable advancement in education. However, it is important to note that this technique was not designed sorely for reading purposes. It can also be used in numerous other creative ways to find solutions to problems and for memorization, to relieve stress, for health improvement, and to a certain extent, for positive thinking.

Quantum Physics and Reading

The term quantum is a word derived from Physics, which means the interaction in which energy changes to light. In quantum speed-reading, the process involves engaging all the elements of the reader and the environment by including interaction with the whole class. In order to accelerate learning, the technique creates synergy by coordinating all the aspects of games, entertainment, positive thinking, emotional intelligence and physical freshness. Before you begin, it is vital to follow some basic guidelines to get you started. First, prepare yourself, minimize any disturbance, sit in a straight up position, and take some time to release the mind.

While this is a completely new technique with little exploration outside Japan, this technique has been proven to reap magnificent results, all documented. However, there have been growing concerns about the topic, and many sources claim that this technique works best in children with an attempt to utilize the right side of the brain. This does not necessarily rule out the possibility of adults learning the technique. It only means that it takes a much longer time to grasp the concept.

Quantum speed-reading, like the other techniques explained, is also a skill that requires plenty of practice to fully master how to use it. Children between the ages of 7 and 12 are best equipped to learn this technique. During quantum reading, the reader is forced to tap into his right hemisphere of the brain in order to take in the information.

Photo Reading

Before going through this technique, first a fact: did you know that your conscious mind is in a position to handle only about seven pieces of information at any one time, while your subconscious mind may handle a breathtaking twenty thousand pieces of information at a go! This is the main difference between normal reading (your average reading speed of 150 to 300 words per minute) and speed-reading. This is the concept applied in Photo Reading. While most people like to use the word "whole" as a replacement of "subconscious" to eliminate the mystery, both words refer to the same thing: bringing together the power of the whole brain to expand its capabilities.

Imagine how much more you can achieve with your brain if you put its full power to use. How much more would you be able to read? The idea behind this technique is to enable a reader to read a text with a staggering speed of 25,000 words per minute by forming a photographic memory of the text. When looking for information, one setback most people encounter is a backlog of information that may or may not be relevant. When you find yourself in this situation, the only way to get the information you want is to go through all the documents, books, articles, and websites and filter what is relevant from what is not. The bad news is, this might take a very long time; time which you could be spending doing other things.

Photo Reading Basics

This is where Photo Reading comes into play. This technique takes advantage of the fact that not all books are equally valuable. Therefore, rather than reading word for word each of the books in front of you, why not use Photo Reading to determine what is useful from the clutter, and what is not. You will find that some books are a complete waste of time, others contain a few useful ideas that you may remember and the rest you completely forget and only a few will leave you hanging onto every word. However, if you do not have the necessary technique to read the columns of information, whether the books are relevant or not, you will still have to read each one of them word by word.

Photo reading solves this problem with a **multi-pass** and **nonlinear method** of reading. Rather than diving blindly into a book reading every word until the end, you make multiple passes through all the books, diving deeper each time until you get to the point of diminishing returns. You will find yourself finishing a book in fifteen minutes at times, (if that is what it takes to extract any important information) and other times 2 hours depending on the content of the book. When reading a typical book, your first pass should take about five minutes. In some cases, this would be the end of your reading, as you would have extracted all the relevant details that are needed, and it would be useless continuing with the rest of the book. Other cases might require you to make extra passes in order for you to squeeze out all the information you might need. This might take you about two hours, on average. The thing about Photo Reading is that, the length of time you spend on a book is directly proportional to its relevance to you. When photo reading, the reader must engage with the information actively in order to improve comprehension.

Since its discovery, Photo Reading has had several successful stories despite the fact that NASA downplayed its effectiveness. As expected, reading at a speed of 25,000 words per minute, as with Photo Reading, requires you to tap into your whole mind using the techniques of Neuro Linguistic Programming (NLP).

Basically, before reading, you should put your mind in a calm and peaceful state, preparing it to absorb the information you are about to take in. You need to make your mind aware that you are going to read at a fast rate in order for it to wait for certain specific information to pick from the text. Many instances require you to read at a higher speed on your day-to-day activities. These include reading magazines and journals, mails and emails, websites and other electronic files, reports, memos, training manuals, notification books, specification sheets, novels, short stories and poetry. If you consider these materials, how would you rate your reading and comprehension rate? More so, how long do you remember the information read? What would you like to change? While some people do not believe that it is possible to read at a speed of 25,000 words per minute, Photo Reading is not a usual method of reading.

Speed Up With Photo Reading

One of the defects of the current education system globally is that it emphasizes on the traditional reading paradigm, which is a very limiting technique that most of us grew up learning with. In order to transition from this kind of thinking, you need to shift from using only the left hemisphere of your brain to incorporate your right side of the brain. The main difference between the two hemispheres of the brain lies in their functions. The left hemisphere is involved in analyzing, sequencing information, and reasoning logically. On the other hand, the work of the right side of the brain is to synthesize, interpret, create internal images, and respond instinctively. When you acknowledge the fact that you can be able to read text fast at more-than-conscious level, you can shift your thinking from the reading paradigm. But how do you do it?

Prepare

In order to read effectively, you need to begin with a clear sense of purpose. State what you want your desired outcome to be in your mind. Someone might want to read just to get an overview of the main points, while another might be reading with an aim of getting specific details like the solution to a certain problem. Alternatively, maybe you want to find some ideas to use in completing a specific task. Purpose plays the role of a radar signal in the internal mind, enabling it produce the desired results. When this has been achieved, you can then enter a state of alertness. In this state, you are neither bored nor anxious. You are under pressure to get results, but you are not worried.

Preview

This step is based primarily on the principle that effective reading usually happens from whole to parts. This means that, in order to get to the finer details, you first consider the bigger picture to get an idea what the material is all about. You do this by running over the text, looking for specific key words that might necessitate deeper reading. When you are through with the text, you then go back to the top, looking for the identified key words. If you find that the keywords in the text are of no value to you, you can then stop reading. The purpose of previewing is to know how the text is organized or structured in order to get a clue as to the content of the material.

Normally, it takes about five minutes to complete a book preview, 3 minutes for a report and a diminishing thirty seconds for an article. You can think of previewing as doing an x-ray. The purpose is same; to get an idea of the structure, in this case, of the bones. When we have this information, we can be able to predict what is coming next. Similarly, when you know how a text is structured, you can be able to predict what you are going to read next and this improves your comprehension rate.

Photo Read

This technique begins by putting your mind in a more calm and relaxed state, otherwise known as the accelerative state of mind. This state is free of worries, distractions, anxiety, and stresses. After this has been achieved, you then prepare your vision for the **Photo Focus state**. This is where you expand your peripheral vision and instead of capturing the text on a word-to-word basis, you adjust your vision to bring the whole printed page into view.

One of the effects of Photo Focus is that it opens your mental and physical window, allowing the passage of the visual stimuli to the brain. When you are in this state, you mentally photograph the whole page and direct it to the preconscious processor of the brain. With each page you expose to the preconscious processor, a direct neurological response is stimulated. The brain does its work of pattern recognition, undisturbed by the thought process and activity of your conscious mind. With speeds of one page per second, you can photo read a book in roughly three to five minutes. However, since your conscious mind is normally unaware of the synthesis of the new information, this means that you will not remember the material from your conscious memory. In order to retrieve this information, you need to tap into your conscious mind and make it aware of the information. This is the next step.

Activate

This process involves re-stimulating the brain by asking questions and dipping into the parts of the passage that we feel most attracted to. You then speed read the rest of the material by quickly scanning down the middle of each column or page of type. When you find it necessary, you dip into those parts of the text that are concentrated with the information you need in order to understand the necessary details. Doing this actually allows your intuition to tell you exactly which page you should be looking for in order to get the information you need. During activation, you engage your whole mind and link the information from your subconscious mind to your conscious level in order to achieve the desired results.

Rapid Read

The purpose of this step is usually to make the information acquired stick to our long-term memory. Rapid reading involves scanning through the whole document after you have photo read it, word for word until the end while adjusting the speed to your desired rate, usually in a bid to remember the information. Most people practice this technique when they are beginning photo reading for fear of forgetting what they have read. Others however skip this step normally because they have already achieved their desired goals. The time taken to finish reading using rapid reading depends on a number of factors:

- Complexity of the material

- Prior knowledge of the information

- The value of the material.

Rapid reading purely involves the conscious mind, and serves to dispel the fear among many beginners that they cannot recall what they have read or worse, the information never sticks.

Part 7:
Reading and Your Short-Term Memory

The short-term memory is the portion of your brain that absorbs information, holds for a short time before it is either discarded or transferred to the long-term memory. The purpose of the short-term memory is to hold information just long enough for you to grasp the details in paper, like when you are memorizing the telephone number of a friend or getting instructions to the nearest hospital. After that, the facts are either overridden by other information or transferred to the long-term memory where they become a permanent part of your knowledge. Reading is the process of acquiring information, holding it in the short-term memory and then, if possible, assimilating it in the long-term memory.

Assimilating Concepts and Ideas

Over the years, researchers have presented several concepts to explain what happens in your brain when reading. They use these to explain the concept of speed-reading i.e. how your brain reorganizes information being received and translates it according to your experiences for you to comprehend it. Below are some of these concepts:

Chunking

Chunking is dividing the information you take in into bite-sized pieces for you to comprehend and retain it much more quickly. The difference between speed-readers and normal readers is that the former have a better ability to retain information and are therefore better chunkers than the average person is. As you know, the short-term memory can only hold five to seven words at a go, and that is what a normal reader relies on. However, a speed-reader can hold up to five to seven thought units (not words), which is what makes the whole difference. This is mainly because a speed-reader does not rely on the conscious memory when reading. Rather, he utilizes the whole brain to activate the right hemisphere, and uses it to subconsciously absorb information.

Pacers

Most people trying speed-reading for the first time normally use a pacer to guide them through the text. A pacer can be anything including a pen, ruler or a pencil that acts a visual aid in speed reading. In your first stages of learning, a pacer might come in handy in many ways. It can guide you through the text, and hide the previous passages that have been covered. However, it is advisable to cease using the pacer once you have grasped the fundamentals of speed-reading. Before reading anything, the best way to ensure that you keep your focus is to determine a purpose for your reading. Different materials will require different types of reading techniques. If you are reading for pleasure, say a novel or a storybook, you are better off reading slowly and luxuriously. On the other hand, if you are reviewing for a test and are running out of time, then you will need the skills of speed-reading.

Purposeful Reading

Having a purpose in mind when reading will determine the level of concentration and speed that you will apply to a given text. There are a couple of questions that you need to ask yourself before reading in order to determine whether to read fast or not. For instance, if you are reading about something that will give a promotion or advance you to a higher level, then you should read slowly and luxuriously, taking your time to grasp the details properly. You could also apply speed-reading techniques, but make sure you underline specific points and details that need special attention. On the other hand, reading a menu does not require any specific level of attention, so you can just scribble through the list as fast as you want.

Reading in Clumps

As emphasized previously, regular reading is a process that involves focusing on one word at a time, until the reader reaches the end of the text. One concept that you will find useful in a bid to increase your reading speed is the use of clumps. When reading in clumps, rather than focusing your eyes on one word at a time, you take in several words at a go. A clump consists of four to sixteen words that are arranged next to each other, and which you take in at a single glance.

One of the benefits of speed-reading is the fact that you cannot stop to vocalize, and as a result, this increases your reading speed. This stands to reason; it is not possible to say four to sixteen words at a go without slurring, or turning the words into corned beef hash! Newspapers are generally arranged in columns, and these columns are clumps in themselves. Holy books too, like the Bible and Koran, are laid out in columns. If you are a religious person who reads holy text, or are a newspaper enthusiast, you already know how to read in clumps. The thing about reading in columns is that they encourage you to read in clumps. This, as a result, increases your reading speed automatically.

Reading in clumps is relatively easy because you use both your peripheral vision and macular vision in the process. Macular vision is what most people call the primary focus. You apply this vision when looking directly at something, thanks primarily to the macula of your eye's retina. Peripheral vision, on the other hand, is what you see outside your macular vision, usually less distinctly. Since the receptor cells are usually concentrated at the center of the retina, it becomes very hard to distinguish colors and shapes in peripheral vision. However, you can see the areas surrounding your macular vision, including the upward, downward, and sideways of its border.

Now, when applying these two visions when reading, your primary focus follows the words directly before the eyes, while the peripheral vision takes in the words horizontally on the right and left. It is not about improving your eyesight. Learning to use your peripheral vision is more like improving your concentration and focus in order to increase both your reading and comprehension rates. Training yourself to use both these visions can significantly improve your overall reading speed.

Things to Remember

Speed Reading Is About Control

Very often, people are tricked into believing that speed reading is some miraculous tool that will help them get through 1000 page books in a single day. While this is certainly achievable with speed reading, I have noticed that there is always too much emphasis placed on the "speed" aspect of it, and not so much on the "comprehension" aspect. That's why so many people who are new to speed reading think that an increase in reading speed obviously means a decrease in your comprehension abilities. They are of the opinion that reading too fast makes you unable to process the data at a similar pace and hence, you lose out on understanding the meaning fully. This is completely false if you truly master speed reading.

Reading faster is not the only thing that speed reading aims to teach you. Speed reading is about having total control of what you are reading and at what speed you do it. It is very much similar to driving a race car in a Grand Prix. Yes, it is really important to achieve the top speed whenever possible and be the fastest car in the race, but it is also equally important to have great control over your speed on the tricky turns and alleys. Imagine if the fastest driver crashed after just the first lap simply because he couldn't control his car at a crucial turn. That would be disastrous, wouldn't it?

This is what I want to get through to the readers of this book. Speed reading is about control. When you are able to control the speed of your reading with ease and can efficiently understand all that the text says, you have truly mastered the art of speed reading. Speed reading isn't just blindly running through the text without any comprehension. It is the exact opposite.

We have already discussed how we can alter the reading speeds in between different parts of the text by using a pointer aid, like a ruler or the index finger. Relying on a pointer aid helps us follow the movement of the pointer to regulate the speed rather than our own eyes, which can be unreliable and inconsistent. So moving your hand faster than normal will result in reading faster while doing the opposite will result in slower reading.

This enables a reader to control the reading speed as required. When going through easy-to-understand parts, one can simply glaze over. On the other hand, when reading complex parts, one can easily slow down and take in all the information carefully.

Know When To Slow Down

It is important to know when you need to slow down while reading, as we have discussed in the previous section. People love to brag about how fast they finished huge books, and this can make you feel inferior. But you must remember that some books are not meant to be read too quickly. If you do that, you will hardly remember any content from the book, and then there wouldn't really be a point to you reading it in the first place.

You must keep in mind that while the low information and fluff parts of the book can be skimmed over faster, the complex and high information parts need to be read carefully and at a moderate speed which allows you to understand everything clearly.

Even more than this, speed reading is not just two extremes of reading: skimming and slow reading. It includes all the different layers of speed we read at to understand different types of content. The speed at which you read poetry will differ from the speed at which you read a novel or the speed at which you read a book on Quantum Mechanics. This is what you need to understand to master speed reading.

Conclusion

Learning to speed read takes time and effort. Don't kid yourself, you will not learn how to read 1000 words or more in one minute in just a day; you need to practice and do more practice and in no time, you will reach 1000 words per minute and even surpass this.

In general, you start speed-reading by first eliminating some of the old reading habits most people use including rescanning over already read pages, sounding out words while reading and other common practices. When these have been dealt with, you can then proceed with the basic techniques, which is running your finger over the text as you read it, and trying not to sound it out. With time, you can then progress your speed slowly until it reaches your desired maximum.

When reading a text, the first rule to observe is that, you should not slow down while reading for any reason; you should maintain a constant speed until you are through. While increasing your speed is crucial when reading documents, social media, books and so forth, an effective speed-reading program should try to match your reading speed with the level of understanding; otherwise, it will just be useless.

Sometimes you will be required to re-read through a text in order to internalize and comprehend effectively, which is perfectly all right. In some instances, you might succeed to improve your speed to about five times that of a normal reader, but fail in comprehension, which is typical of most speed-readers. Some generally scan through a text but fail to understand what it means completely, which can be hazardous to learning. Aside from these setbacks, speed reading is an essential skill that can complement normal reading, since there are some things that the brain cannot do while scanning or skimming that take place when speed reading.

Key Takeaways from This Book

- Speed reading takes time to learn so don't be frustrated that you have not increased your speed within a week. Keep on practicing.

- You cannot use all the techniques mentioned to increase your speed; some will work for you and some that will not.

- Speed reading's effectiveness differs depending on the circumstances.

How to Put This Information into Action

- First, you need to understand the various speed reading techniques so that you can choose one that works best for you.

- You would also need to eliminate one by one the old habits you do when reading.

- It is also important that as you learn to speed read, you improve your comprehension.

- What about trying speed-reading on this book, for starters? Use various techniques and find out which ones work best for you. Good luck!

Resources for Further Viewing And Reading

Recommended Websites

- Iris Reading: http://www.irisreading.com/speed-reading/simple-speed-reading-tip-use-your-hand/

- Mind Tools: http://www.mindtools.com/speedrd.html

- Street Directory: http://www.streetdirectory.com/etoday/speed-reading-made-easy-pfaujf.html

- Ace Reader: www.acereader.com/articles/

- Huffington Post: www.huffingtonpost.ca/2013/01/08/how-to-speed-read_n_2433415.html

Recommended Blogs

- Life Hacker: http://lifehacker.com/the-truth-about-speed-reading-1542508398

- Speed Reading Tips: http://speedreadingtips.blogspot.com/

- Scotthyoung: www.scotthyoung.com/blog/2007/03/10/double-your-reading-rate/

- IQ Matrix: http://blog.iqmatrix.com/increase-reading-speed

- The Speed Reading
  Coach: www.thespeedreadingcoach.com/blog/

Did You Like Speed Reading Simplified?

Before you leave, I wanted to say thank-you again for buying my book.

I know you could have picked from a number of different books on this topic, but you chose this one so I can't thank-you enough for doing that and reading until the end.

I'd like to ask you a small favor.

If you enjoyed this book or feel that it has helped you in anyway, then could you please take a minute and post an honest review about it on Amazon?

Your review will help get my book out there to more people and they'll be forever grateful, as will I.

Preview of "Brain Training NOW: A Fun Guide to Training Your Brain, Improving Your Memory and Increasing Your Attention"

Chapter 4:
Cognitive Exhaustion

Complete Breathing

In order for the body to be fully healthy, aside from the essential water and food, air is important. Humans are capable of surviving without food for several weeks but just a few days without water. However, humans cannot survive without clean air to breathe. Life begins and stops with just a single breath.

In breathing, there are 3 different phases that have to be distinguished:

- Inhalation

- Exhalation

- Pause in breathing

The first phase flows into the other without stopping. Each exhalation should be about twice as long as the inhalation and the pause should arise naturally once the exhalation phase is done. The impulse to inhale should then arise naturally. This is what is known as the "Full Yoga Breath" or Complete Breathing. This is known as the source of life. The inhalation is the phase that forms the active part of breathing. The respiratory muscles contract during this phase, while in the exhalation, the muscles relax.

Deep, quiet, and regular breathing is needed in order for a person to become healthy. Complete breathing has a calming and harmonizing effect to the well-being of a person. When breathing is rapid and shallow, the effects are the opposite: tension, nervousness, pain, and stress are felt. A common mistake in breathing is that the abdomen is drawn in when the chest starts to expand rather than letting the abdomen relax forwards. Deep breathing is impaired when you draw your abdomen in. Wearing restrictive clothing also inhibits the natural movements involved in deep breathing.

In Yoga, all exercises, including breathing exercises, should be done slowly and without the extra tension. Breathing should be silent and done through the nose. The air is filtered, warmed, and moistened this way. With all of the exercises in Yoga, it is important that everything is practiced in a state that is physically and mentally relaxed. The muscles can stretch better without any tension when the body is physically relaxed. A mentally relaxed state will help a person to practice the breathing exercises with complete concentration.

What is Cognitive Exhaustion?

The brain, just like with any other organ, also gets exhausted from time to time. Just similar to a computer, the brain also crashes when it receives too much stress. The brain may experience exhaustion at different times, depending on how much stress that a person gets. On a normal day with just the right amounts of stress, cognitive exhaustion would usually occur at the end of the day. But if the brain gets too much stress early on in the day and cannot find a way to relax, cognitive exhaustion may develop any time.

Cognitive exhaustion is a special type of tiredness or fatigue that is common among those who have suffered from a mild to severe injury to the brain. When a person suffers from cognitive exhaustion, his or her brain has to exert more effort in order to be able to concentrate better on tasks that are normally easy to do. This type of fatigue can also lead to the development of learning difficulties, behavioral problems, as well as mood swings.

The following symptoms are commonly found:

- One finds it difficult to maintain attention.

- One does not have the endurance for various thinking tasks.

- The person may be able to concentrate at first but would lose concentration over time.

- Thinking tasks are very difficult to continue.

- The person needs to sleep more or needs to take a nap in order to continue the day.

- The behavior of the person is very different when he or she is well rested and fresh compared to when he or she is tired.

- Headaches are also rampant.

- People tend to trudge on the day and eventually become exhausted by the end of the day.

- There are behavioral difficulties that arise, such as irritability, feeling miserable, or hyperactivity.

Cognitive Exhaustion Techniques

There are actually ways on how to fight cognitive exhaustion. These are also good ways on how to prevent the onset of cognitive exhaustion in the future. Here are the different techniques on how to combat cognitive exhaustion:

1. *Body Balance*

Eating a hearty and good breakfast, getting an apple instead of a candy bar, and going to bed early are all ways on how to achieve balance in your body. Once you think that you are already experiencing a lot of stress, think of this: "This too shall pass!" Drinking at least 8 glasses of water a day will help a person not to be dehydrated chronically. Being dehydrated chronically actually depletes one's energy. Exercise also helps to keep the mind relaxed, so one way of achieving this is by taking the stairs at work instead of the elevator.

2. *Brain Drain Remedy – Zen Style*

Freeing the mind and the emotions is important as there are habits that could drain the energy. There are burdens that you may be carrying mentally that keep you from being mentally present in certain situations. As one saying goes, you may be "physically present but mentally absent." Remember that you have the capacity to make a choice where your attention should be focused on.

3. Getting Rid of Emotional Vampires.

Scientists have proven that emotions are contagious. Have you seen how one person who panics can cause other people in a room to panic as well? There are mirror neurons in the body that get triggered so that you directly experience what other people are also experiencing. Make a list of the people you know that drain you emotionally and mentally. Be sure to cut off toxic relationships, and instead, focus on having positive ones. Prevent from living the superhuman lifestyle as well. Learn when to say no. Set your priorities straight.

4. Renewal of the Spiritual Aspect of Your Life.

The main challenge of making changes in your life is living with the changes. This would mean having to tap into an energy source within one's self that will push you. Think of this: at the end of the day, what values or qualities do you wish to abide by? You will be able to live a life that is filled with joy this way.

5. Practicing the Qigong Breath

Stand with your feet apart (about hip-distance), arms at the sides, and the knees relaxed. As you slowly inhale, raise your arms slowly towards the sides with your palms up. Imagine that you are a person trying to gather the energy of the earth then the sky. Continue until your hands are over your head. As you lower your hands, exhale, with your palms down in front. As you are exhaling, imagine that the natural energy around you is flowing through you that cleanses, relaxes, and revitalizes your emotions, body, and mind. Continue doing this for 3 minutes.

6. *Love Blast*

First, you have to picture the face of a person or a pet that you love. Studies have shown that this type of visualization actually releases a lot of chemicals that help you feel good, such as endorphins. This will then help boost your energy. This practice can help nourish your spirit, body, and heart, which can then help reshape your life.

How Cognitive Exhaustion Techniques Work

Cognitive exhaustion techniques work by helping the mind become more relaxed. A relaxed mind, as emphasized in previous chapters, helps a person be calm. This will help him or her make decisions better. These exercises also help you to build up your energy significantly.

More Books You Might Like

Household DIY: *Save Time and Money with Do It Yourself Hints and Tips on Furniture, Clothes, Pests, Stains, Residues, Odors and More!*

DIY Household Hacks: *Save Time and Money with Do It Yourself Tips and Tricks for Cleaning Your House*

Essential Oils: Essential Oils & Aromatherapy for Beginners: *Proven Secrets to Weight Loss, Skin Care, Hair Care & Stress Relief Using Essential Oil Recipes*

Apple Cider Vinegar for Beginners: *An Apple Cider Vinegar Handbook with Proven Secrets to Natural Weight Loss, Optimum Health and Beautiful Skin*

Body Butter Recipes: *Proven Formula Secrets to Making All Natural Body Butters that Will Hydrate and Rejuvenate Your Skin*

68014201R00047

Made in the USA
Lexington, KY
28 September 2017